Assurance
By Thomas Goodwin
Edited by Kevin Hay

© 2022 by Kevin Hay

Published by: H&E Publishing, West Lorne, Ontario, Canada
www.hesedandemet.com

Classics in Biblical Spiriutality Series Editor: Dustin Benge

All rights reserved. This book or any portion thereof may not be reproduced or used in any manner whatsoever without the express written permission of the publisher except for the use of brief quotations in a book review.

Thomas Goodwin, "Christ Set Forth," in *The Works of Thomas Goodwin*, vol. 4, (Edinburgh: James Nichol, 1862).

Scripture quotations are from The ESV® Bible (The Holy Bible, English Standard Version®), copyright © 2001 by Crossway, a publishing ministry of Good News Publishers. Used by permission. All rights reserved.

Cover painting: *The Rocky Mountains* by Albert Bierstadt

Design and layout: Dustin Benge

Paperback ISBN: 978-1-77484-076-4
Ebook ISBN: 978-1-77484-077-1

First edition, 2022

ASSURANCE

Our Confidence in Christ

THOMAS GOODWIN

Edited by Kevin Hay

CONTENTS

Biography: The Life and Ministry of Thomas Goodwin		7
Preface		11
Introduction		15
1	Confidence in Christ's Life	19
2	Confidence in Christ's Death	29
3	Confidence in Christ's Resurrection	39
4	Confidence in Christ's Ascension	55
5	Confidence in Christ's Intercession	71

"Let us draw near with a true heart in full assurance of faith, with our hearts sprinkled clean from an evil conscience and our bodies washed with pure water."

HEBREWS 10:22

BIOGRAPHY

The Life and Ministry of Thomas Goodwin

Thomas Goodwin was born on October 5, 1600, in Rollesby, Norfolk. Goodwin's entrance into the world was marked by meager beginnings. Not only was Rollesby a small village near Yarmouth, but Goodwin himself was born prematurely. As the oldest son to godly parents, Goodwin was raised in a Christian home and was provided a robust classical education. With the goal of seeing their son become a pastor, the educational investment of Goodwin's parents seemed to pay off, as he entered college at just 12 years of age.

On August 25, 1613, Thomas Goodwin began his university education at Christ's College, in Cambridge. He excelled in the realm of academia as a proven scholar, graduating with a B.A. in 1616. By his own admission, though, the desires of his heart were hedonistic and self-seeking. Motivated by the honor of men, Goodwin's goal was to become a famous preacher who would be known for his great intellectual and oratorical abilities. Therefore, with that purpose as the driving influence of his life, the young Thomas Goodwin studied diligently and stood out among his peers.

Simultaneously, Goodwin was being exposed to the teaching and preaching of the Puritans. Cambridge had been greatly impacted by the preaching ministry of William Perkins, and other Puritans were instrumental in the spiritual instruction taking place while Goodwin was attending there. Among them, Richard Sibbes and John Preston stood out distinctively, as both pastors and preachers.

Thomas Goodwin struggled mightily, for quite some time, to find the objective assurance of his salvation. After a lengthy period of wrestling with God, Goodwin eventually came away with a blessing from the Lord, and it produced in him a radical transformation. This transformation was evident in every aspect of his life, especially in the mortification of his flesh, the proclamation of God's Word, and the reformation of his theological beliefs.

In 1619, Goodwin moved to Catherine Hall, and in 1620 was elected as a Fellow there. By 1625, he had become a licensed preacher of the University. Then, following the death of Richard Sibbes, he took over as preacher of Holy Trinity Church. And, in 1630 he obtained the degree of B.D.

Goodwin worked hard in his preaching ministry, no longer for the purpose of becoming honored and renowned for his speaking abilities, but rather, to contend for the spiritual health and vitality of the souls entrusted to him. His ministry enjoyed much success until the year 1634, when he resigned his lectureship position of Holy Trinity Church to become a Congregationalist preacher.

Although the years immediately following his departure are a mystery, in 1638 Goodwin married Elizabeth Prescot of London. Just one year later, in 1639, he and his new bride fled to Holland to escape persecution. However, his preaching ministry did not stop. Goodwin initially settled in Amsterdam, and then to Arnhem, but all the while he continued to fellowship with like-minded believers and to minister to God's people. Soon, Goodwin was able to relocate back to London, and there he began pastoring an Independent congregation, which he enjoyed for ten fruitful years. During this time, in God's providence, Goodwin became well known for his preaching.

Then, in 1643, Goodwin was chosen to become a member of the Westminster Assembly, where he identified as an Independent, and was regularly known, alongside others, as "dissenting brethren." He was frequently asked to preach at the House of Commons, which led to his appointment to become president of Magdalen College, in

Oxford, in 1650. Goodwin maintained this position until the year 1660. He also served as chaplain to Oliver Cromwell, beginning in 1656.

From 1660 until the end of his life, at the age of 80 years old, Goodwin worked alongside other notable men, such as John Owen. He also dedicated himself to the study of theology, but above all, Thomas Goodwin's life demonstrated that he was a pastor at heart.

PREFACE

Kevin Hay

While attending Christ's College, in Cambridge, a teenage Thomas Goodwin was anxiously preparing to take communion for the second time. In doing so, he firmly believed that it would confirm him in the faith so fully that he would never be able to fall away. In the midst of his own misconceptions, however, he was refused communion on the basis of his age. This experience of humiliation and public rejection so disoriented Thomas Goodwin that it threw him into a spiritual tailspin.

Then, on October 2, 1620, just three days before his twentieth birthday, Goodwin providentially heard a funeral sermon by Thomas Bainbridge that brought him to the sincere conviction of his own sin. This conviction would eventually lead to his genuine conversion to Christ. Even then, though, Goodwin experienced the restlessness of his own soul. Thomas Goodwin was on a quest for assurance, but much of his searching was taking place inwardly. Like a thorough detective, Goodwin searched diligently for clues and attempted to examine the evidence of his own salvation by looking within. Rather than finding a secure resting place for his soul, however, he experienced perpetual anxiety of his spirit. The problem was that Goodwin was attempting to set his soul upon an ever—changing object, which was the subjective status of his own progress in sanctification.

That all changed, however, when Goodwin shared his anxieties with a pastor and friend named Mr. Price. After hearing Goodwin articulate his apprehensions, Price provided his good friend with wise, biblical counsel: "Stop looking to your own life for assurance and look to Christ!"

This single truth would prove to be one of the greatest means of transformation in Goodwin's life. Not only did it provide rest for his soul while he lived, but it also prepared him for the day of his death. As he would testify on his death bed:

> I am going to the three Persons, with whom I have had communion: they have taken me; I did not take them. I shall be changed in the twinkling of an eye, all my lusts and corruptions I shall be rid of, which I could not be here; those croaking toads will fall off

in a moment... I could not have imagined I should ever have had such a measure of faith in this hour; no, I could never have imagined it. My bow abides in strength. Is Christ divided? No, I have the whole of his righteousness; I am found in him, not in my own righteousness, which is of the law, but in the righteousness which is of God, which is by faith of Jesus Christ, who loved me and gave himself for me. Christ cannot love me better than he doth; I think I cannot love Christ better than I do; I am swallowed up in God."[1]

---

[1] Thomas Goodwin, *The Works of Thomas Goodwin*, vol. 2 (Edinburgh: James Nichol, 1861–1866), lxxiv–lxxv..

"I write these things to you who believe in the name of the Son of God, that you may know that you have eternal life."

1 JOHN 5:13

INTRODUCTION

Thomas Goodwin

Throughout my life, I have witnessed many holy and precious souls who have clearly and completely given themselves to Christ and have trusted in Christ alone for their justification. Yet, in the ordinary course and way of their lives, these souls have been overly focused on the fundamentals of Christ in their own hearts, and not after Christ himself. Rather, the stream of their focus and deepest intentions has run in the channel of self-reflection, and searching into the gracious inclinations of their own hearts, they only find brief sights of Christ. Yet, as Romans 10:8 says, Christ himself is "near them" if they would simply look upon him with thoughts of pure and singular faith.

And although God allows us to examine our faithfulness

as an evidence of our salvation, the minds of many are overly focused on their own hearts. But let these consider what a dishonor this must necessarily be to Christ, that his train and our faithfulness should have a fuller court and more frequent attendance from our hearts than himself, who is the "King of Glory." And likewise, what a shame also it is for believers themselves, who are his bride, to only look at their husband's reflection or at him indirectly through the intervention and assistance of their own faithfulness as mediators between him and them.

Now to correct this error, the way is not to completely reject all use of such evidences, but to order them, both for the season, and the application of them. Thus whenever we would go down into our own hearts, and take a view of our faithfulness, let us be sure first to look completely out of ourselves to Christ as our justification. If we see our faith clinging to Christ as he sits upon his throne of grace, with the evidences of our salvation coming in like handmaids to attend and witness to the truth of our faith, then we can conclude that our faith in Christ is genuine.

Now to help believers in this way, my goal is to provide Christ to all believers as the object of our faith and the cause of our justification. In doing so, my hope is that you will see what abundant provision God has laid up in Christ for all believers to live upon. I want you to discover everything in Christ, in both his person and his work, with a joint voice speaking justification to us. It is only after presenting Christ in his life, death, resurrection, ascension, and in his sitting in heaven, performing the intercession of his priesthood, that we can truly begin to appreciate how Christ's heart, now in heaven, stands moved to us sinners here below. The Father of our Lord Jesus Christ grant us according to the riches of his glory, that Christ may dwell in our hearts by faith, and that we may know the love of Christ which passes knowledge! Amen.

"Who shall bring any charge against God's elect? It is God who justifies."

ROMANS 8:33

ONE

Confidence in Christ's Life

The words uttered by the Apostle Paul, in Romans 8:33–34, are a triumphing declaration in the name of all the elect. He begins it by saying, "Who shall bring any charge against God's elect? It is God who justifies." And then he follows those words by saying, "Who is to condemn?" namely, God's elect. "Christ Jesus is the one who died." This declaration is first found proclaimed by Jesus Christ himself, our only champion, in Isaiah 50:8 (a chapter made of and for Christ), which says, "He who vindicates me is near. Who will contend with me?" These words were spoken of God's justifying Christ, but they are also applicable to every believer whom God justifies. Christ is brought in uttering these words while standing at the high priest's tribunal. While being beat and spit upon, he was condemned by Pilate and then exercised this faith on God his father saying, "He who vindicates me is near."

And just as he stood in our place during his condemnation, so in this hope of his justification he speaks in our place as our representative in both. And upon this the apostle pronounces here, in similar words, of all the elect, "It is God who justifies; who shall bring any charge?" Christ was condemned, yes, "who died; who is to condemn?" Therefore, may we behold the communion we have with Christ in his death and condemnation, but also in his very faith. Just as Christ trusted in God, so must we, and just as certainly be delivered.

Christ: The Example of Faith
The Faith of Christ for Himself
First, in some sense Christ had a faith for justification like ours, though not a justification through faith as we have. He did not go outside of himself to rely on another for righteousness, for he had enough of his own (since he is "the Lord our righteousness"). Yet he believes on God to justify him, and had recourse to God for justification. "He is near" (he says) "that vindicates me." If he stood simply in his own person, and merely upon his own foundation, there would have been no reason for such a speech. And yet consider him as he stood in our stead. What need would there have been for such a justification apart from condemnation? Therefore, Christ must be supposed to

stand here (in Isaiah) at God's tribunal, as well as at Pilate's, with all our sins upon him. And so the same prophet tells us, "the Lord has laid on him the iniquity of us all" (Isa. 53:6). Christ was made sin and a curse, and therefore he not only stood in danger of Pilate's condemnation, but also of God's, unless he satisfied him for all those sins. And when the wrath of God for sin came upon him, Christ exercised faith to trust and wait on God for his justification. He trusted God to remove those sins and his wrath and to be satisfied and acquitted.

For Christ, his deliverance and justification from all these would be given to him at his resurrection. As Psalm 16 says (a psalm about Christ suffering and lying in the grave), "I have set the Lord always before me; because he is at my right hand, I shall not be shaken. Therefore my heart is glad, and my whole being rejoices; my flesh also dwells secure. For you will not abandon my soul to Sheol;" that is, under the load of these sins, and your wrath laid on me for them; "or let your holy one see corruption" (Ps. 16:8–10). This is in line with what is said in this one word, "He is near that vindicates me," for Christ's resurrection was a justification of him, as I will proceed to show.

The Faith of Christ for Us
Second, neither did Christ exercise faith for himself only, but also for us, and in a greater way than any of us have. In dying and emptying himself, Christ trusted God with the

merit of all his sufferings in advance for the thousands of souls that would be saved through him a long while after, even to the end of the world. He died and trusted all that merit into his Father's hands to provide grace and glory to all those for whom he died. And this is a greater trust (considering the infinite number of his elect who had yet to come) than any man has occasion to put forward for himself alone. God trusted Christ before he came into the world and saved many millions of the Jews upon his mere word. And then Christ, at his death, trusts God again as much, both for the salvation of Jews and Gentiles that were to believe after his death.

In Hebrews 2:12–15, the argument is made that Christ was a man like us, because he lived by faith like we do (which the angels do not). To this end, the apostle brings in these words prophesied of him, as spoken by him of himself, "I will put my trust in him," as one proof that he was a man like us. Now for what was it that he trusted God? By the context it appears to be this: that he should be the salvation of his "brothers" and "children," and raise up a church to God to praise him in.

Application
How should the consideration of these things increase our faith, encourage us, and raise up our hearts above all doubts and withdrawings of spirit in believing? For in this example of Christ's life, we have the highest instance of

believing that ever was. Christ trusted God for himself, and for all his elect. Do you not have the heart to trust him for one poor soul? Yes, Christ trusted God upon his single union. But we, for our assurance, have both Christ and God united to us, even God with Christ as his guarantee (for he is God's guarantee as well as ours). A double union from two such persons, whom will it not secure? Therefore, if God the Father and God the Son mutually trusted one another for salvation, whom would it not cause to trust them both for our own salvation, especially when damnation is the alternative?

First, this example of Christ's life should teach and motivate us to believe. For did Christ not lay down all his glory, empty himself, allow himself to be treated as worthless, and surrender all he had into his Father's hands, while trusting that God would cause many to be accounted as righteous (Isa. 53)? Therefore, should we not also lay down all we have, part with whatever is dear to us, in Christlike submission, with complete dependence and hope that we would be justified by him?

Second, this example of Christ's life should also encourage us to believe, especially against the greatness of sins. Do you experience the guilt of innumerable transgressions coming in and discouraging you from trusting in him? Consider what Christ had that was not of his own. Christ was made the greatest sinner that ever was by imputation, for the sins of all God's chosen were placed on him. Yet, he trusted God to be justified from them all, and to be raised up from under the wrath due to them. Ah! You are but one poor sinner, and your faith has but a light and small load upon it, namely, your own sins, which Christ took on himself fully, and is but a fraction of the infinite number he satisfied.

Answering Objections
But you will say, Christ was Christ, one personally united to God, so he knew that he could satisfy him, but I am a sinful man. Well, if you believe, and are united to Christ, then Christ speaking these words in the name of both himself and of his elect gives you the very same basis to utter them that he had. And all that encouraged him may embolden you, because he took your place. His confidence, then, may be your confidence now. His was in and from himself, but yours must be on him. Therefore, by your communion with him in both his condemnation and justification, you may take all that emboldened him and use it to bring you assurance. In addition, you have an aspect of encouragement to your faith that he did not have. Christ has finished the work and fully performed the satisfaction he set out to accomplish.

But you will yet say, he knew himself to be the Son of God, but I do not. Well, if you cast yourself upon him, to be adopted and justified by him, surrendering your soul to be saved in his own way, the same is true for you. And as for that great and persistent discouragement against poor souls, namely, the weight and multitude of our sins, considering the faith of Christ helps to alleviate and remove it more than anything else. For Christ, in bearing the sins of his elect, took on infinitely more sins than yours. And yet you see how confident he was in doing so and how he is now clearly justified from them all. And by virtue of being justified from all sorts of sins, likewise will all sorts of sinners be justified in and through him. Therefore, should you not also hope to be justified from yours?

Christ: The Object of Faith
In Joint Commission with God the Father

The fact that God is the One who justifies, and that Christ is the one who died, are both set forth as the foundation of a believer's confidence (Rom. 8:33–34). Therefore, faith should have an eye on both, for both contribute to the justification of a sinner. It is Christ who paid the price and who performed the righteousness by which we are justified, and it is God who accepts it and who imputes it to us. Therefore, justification is ascribed to both. We also see this in Romans 3:24, which says that we "are justified by his grace as a gift, through the redemption that is in Christ Jesus." So we discover that God's free grace and Christ's righteousness do accomplish our justification.

In Opposition to Our Own Humiliation and Faithfulness

We are not to trust or rest in our humiliation, as many do. That promise, "Come to me, all who labor and are heavy laden, and I will give you rest," has been often mistaken (Matt. 11:28). Many have understood it, as if Christ had spoken peace and rest apart from trusting in him. In actuality, if you are weary, you may have rest indeed, but you must come to Christ first.

Secondly, we are not to rest in our own evidences or efforts. Our faithfulness cannot satisfy our own consciences, much less God's justice. If "righteousness were through" these, then "Christ died for no purpose" (Gal. 2:21). What a dishonor it would be to Christ, that our faithfulness should share any of the glory of his righteousness! Was your faithfulness crucified for you? Faithfulness is the daughter of faith, the offspring of Christ, and it may in time of need nourish its mother, but it is never her source.

In Distinction to the Promises of Forgiveness

Christ's person, and not merely the promises of forgiveness, is to be the object of faith. There are many poor souls humbled by their sin, and removed from their own foundation, who, like Noah's dove, fly all over the word of God, to spy out what they may set their foot upon. Seeing many free and gracious promises which hold out forgiveness of sins and justification in God's word, they immediately settle upon them, and rest on them alone, apart from trusting in Christ. This is a common error among people and is like Noah's dove resting upon the outside of the ark instead of coming to Noah inside. Though she might have been able to rest there for a while, she could not have stayed there to ride out all the storms, but instead, would have perished there in the end.

We may observe that the first promise given was not a mere word simply promising forgiveness, or other benefits which God would bestow. Rather, it was a promise of Christ's person as overcoming Satan, and purchasing those benefits. The seed of the woman was promised to crush the serpent's head (Gen. 3:15). So when the promise was renewed to Abraham, it was not a mere promise of blessedness and forgiveness, but of that seed, that is Christ, in whom that blessedness was conveyed (Gal. 3:16).

The promise is but the chest, and Christ is the jewel in it. The promise is but the field, and Christ is the pearl hid in it, to be chiefly looked at. The promises are the means by which you believe, not the substance upon which you are to rest. Therefore, although you are to look at forgiveness as held forth in the promise, you are to believe on Christ in that promise to obtain this forgiveness.

Now this is the purpose of all the promises: they are all anchored on Christ, in whom they are "yes" and "amen," so you must trust in them through him. There are three sorts of promises, and in applying them all, it is Christ who is the object upon whom our faith rests:

ASSURANCE

First, there are *absolute promises*, made without condition, as when Christ "came to save sinners" (1 Tim. 1:15). Now in these it is plain that Christ is the pure object of them; so that if you do not apply him, you apply nothing, for the only thing held forth in them is Christ.

Next, there are *inviting promises*; like the aforementioned, "Come to me, you that are heavy laden." The promise is not primarily about curing weariness, but about coming to Christ. Those who come to Christ will find rest.

Finally, there are *assuring promises*; as those made regarding certain qualifications of sanctification. But still, what is it that is promised in them, which should captivate the gaze of our heart? It is Christ, in whom the soul rests and finds comfort. In this way, the grace a man experiences is but a backdoor to let faith in and to converse with Christ, whom the soul loves.

TWO

Confidence in Christ's Death

The Divine Attraction

Not only is Christ's life the justifying object of our faith, but so too is Christ's death. Some mistakenly believe that they should look only upon the personal excellencies of grace and glory which are in Jesus Christ and which flow from the hypostatic union. However, the first view a humble soul must see is that of Christ as Savior, who was made sin, a curse, and obedient to death for sinners. Though the gospel certainly presents Christ in his personal excellencies, true belief first sees him under the "likeness of sinful flesh," and in this way he is made a fitting object for a sinner's faith to trust and rest upon for salvation (Rom. 8:3).

Faith here views him not only as glorious at God's right hand, but as crucified, as made sin, and a curse, and so rests upon him for pardon. It is therefore Christ that is thus excellent in his person, yet even more so as clothed with his garments of blood, and the qualifications of a mediator and reconciler. This is what makes him so desirable by sinners and a fitting object for their faith.

It is true that there are various ways to think about faith in Christ. Faith that is carried forth to Christ and his personal excellencies may be called *uniting* faith; faith that goes forth to Christ for strength of grace to subdue sin may be called *sanctifying* faith; and faith as it goes forth to Christ, as dying for justification, may be called *justifying* faith. For faith in that act looks at what Christ does to justify a sinner, and in his dying and rising Christ becomes the most pleasing and grateful object to a humbled soul.

This is why Paul, in his epistle to the Corinthians, determined to "know nothing but Jesus Christ and him crucified" (1 Cor. 2:2). Christ crucified was the Christ they needed above all. Likewise, in Romans, the focus was on a "propitiation by his blood, to be received by faith," because Christ, as shedding his blood for the remission of sins, is the object of it (Rom. 3:25).

Therefore, since "we have redemption through his blood, the forgiveness of sins," Christ's person gives us possession of all the promises, and his blood shows the scope of their power (Eph. 1:7, Col. 1:14). And as sin is the strength of the law, which promises to condemn, so Christ's satisfaction is the strength of all the promises in the gospel. In a word, a humbled soul has access to that Christ who is now alive and glorified in heaven, as the person from whom he is to receive forgiveness, but also as the one who was crucified and made sin.

The Divine Design

Another vital focal point for our faith in Christ's death is the purpose, significance, and intention of God and Christ for his sufferings. The crucifixion is not simply a tragic story of his death. It is the heart and mind and intent of Christ in suffering, which faith primarily looks to, and which increasingly draws the heart to rest on Christ crucified. When a believer sees that Christ's aim in suffering for poor sinners agrees and satisfies the aim and desires of his heart, and that Christ was intent to accomplish it, this draws his heart to rest in and upon Christ. Without this, the contemplation and meditations of the story of his sufferings, and the greatness of them, will be altogether unprofitable. Saving, justifying faith focuses upon the main scope and thrust of Christ's sufferings, because it is in and through them that we obtain forgiveness from our sins in Christ crucified.

As God looks principally at the meaning of the Spirit in prayer (Rom. 8:27), so does faith look principally to the meaning of Christ in his sufferings. You may also observe that the emphasis of all the apostles' epistles is to show the intent of Christ's sufferings: how he was set forth to be "a propitiation for our sins" (1 John 2:2); to "bear our sins upon the tree" (1 Pet. 2:24); and to be "made sin who knew no sin, so that in him we might become the righteousness of God" (2 Cor. 5:21). In like manner, the evangelical prophet, Isaiah, primarily set forth the intent of Christ's sufferings for justification (Isaiah 53), just as David had done before in the story of his passion (Psalm 22). Therefore, to show the use and purpose of his sufferings, the scope of all the apostles' sermons set forth the intent of Christ's passion to be the justification and salvation to sinners.

"The saying is trustworthy and deserving of full acceptance, that Christ Jesus came into the world to save sinners" (1 Tim. 1:15). The purpose of God's ancient design for the sufferings of Christ was an end higher than men or angels had ever conceived. Thus, genuine faith takes it up and gazes upon it. This is the reality upon which Peter sought to anchor the faith of his audience (Acts 2). In doing so, he set forth the heinousness of their sin in murdering "the Lord of life," and then he sought to raise up their hearts again with the goal of helping them to see God's divine purpose so that they might be drawn to believe. He tells them that all this was done "according to the definite plan and foreknowledge of God" (Acts 2:23) for an even greater end than they imagined, even for the remission of sins through his name. It was not the hatred of the Jews, the hypocrisy of Judas, the fearfulness of Pilate, or the sinfulness of the time period that brought about Christ's death, so much as God the Father, collaborating with Christ himself, to accomplish a greater purpose than them all.

The death of Christ was the greatest and strangest design that God ever set out to accomplish and act upon, and therefore he surely had a purpose in proportion to it. The God who "takes no pleasure in the death of the wicked" (Ezek. 33:11) would not will the death of his own Son, whom he loves more than all his creation, if it were for an inferior purpose. Therefore, it must necessarily be some great matter for which God would ordain the death of his holy and innocent Son. Neither could it be any other matter than to destroy that which he most hates, which is sin, and to set forth what he most delights in, which is mercy.

Therefore, may our faith look primarily to this divine design and plan of God, and of Christ in his suffering to satisfy our sins and to justify us sinners. May we behold him as "the Lamb of God who takes away the sins of the world" (John 1:29), and seeing him upon the cross, may our faith behold the sins of us all placed upon him. "Surely he has born our griefs and carried our sorrows" (Isa. 53:4). "He himself bore our sins in his body on the tree" (1 Pet. 2:24) and "was sacrificed once to take away the sins of many" (Heb. 9:28). This purpose of Christ in all that he did and suffered is that welcome news, and the very spirit of the gospel, which faith seeks and rests upon.

The Divine Triumph

Now, having directed your faith to the right object, which is Christ in his death, let us also see what matter of support and encouragement faith may retrieve from his death for justification. Surely, that which has long ago satisfied God himself for the sins of many thousand souls now in heaven, may very well serve to satisfy the heart and conscience of any sinner now upon earth, regardless of the guilt of any sins that can arise. We see that the apostle Paul, after the large discourse on justification by Christ's righteousness (Romans 5), having shown how it abounds in every way, now sits down, as it were, like a man superbly convinced. "What then shall we say to these things?" (Rom. 8:31). He speaks as one satisfied, and even astonished with an abundance of evidence, having nothing to say, but only to admire God and Christ in this work and therefore presently throws down the gauntlet and challenges a dispute with any who would wish to contend. Let conscience and carnal reason, law and sin, hell and devils, bring in all their strength. "Who shall bring any charge against God's elect?" "Who is to condemn?" Paul dares to answer them all and carry it with these few words: "It is God who justifies. It is Christ who died" (Rom. 8:33–34).

Christ's redemption is not merely a ransom, or making the necessary satisfaction according to the just shortcoming of sin, but it is "plentiful redemption" (Ps. 130:7). There is an abundance of grace and "the free gift of righteousness" (Rom. 5:17). There is found the "unsearchable riches of Christ" (Eph. 3:8). In 1 Timothy 1:14, we find Paul saying that "the grace of our Lord *overflowed*." But the word reaches farther than that. Paul's point was to say that as "blasphemer" (1 Tim. 1:13), one might think that he had enough sins to exhaust God's grace, but the reality was that he found so much grace in Christ, it was even more than he knew what to do with.

Therefore, what is there that can be said to magnify sin in the general, or of any man's particular sins, that may not be remedied with the words, "Christ has died"?

First, is sin the transgression of the law? Christ, the lawmaker, was subjected to the law, so will his dying not make amends? Is sin the debasement of God's glory, manifested in his word and works? Christ's dying was the debasement and emptying of the brightness of his glory in the highest measure, as God was personally manifested in the flesh. Sin's highest evil lies in offending God, but Christ's righteousness is the righteousness of God himself.

Second, what peculiar aggravations or circumstances are there in your sins, to weigh you down, that are not met by some circumstance in Christ's obedience and death, that can lift you up again? Look into the heart of Jesus Christ dying, and behold him struggling with his Father's wrath, and you will find the sufferings of his soul more than those of his body, and in them a place to rest in the soul of his sufferings.

Third, is your sin magnified by the fact that you committed it with great delight and self-indulgence, and poured your heart out to it? Consider that Christ offered himself more willingly than you ever did in your sin. And though he showed how miserable it would be to receive God's wrath, since it was his Father's will for our salvation, he joyfully embraced and drank of that cup to the very bottom.

Fourth, did you sin with much deliberation when you could have avoided it? In the circumstances of Christ's sufferings, he knew all he was to suffer, and yet surrendered himself to it.

Fifth, have you sinned presumptuously and made a covenant with death and hell? Christ offered himself up by a covenant and collaborated with his Father to do so.

Sixth, has the name of God been scandalized while holding a high position in the church? Well, how great a position did Christ hold? Even equal with God the Father and yet how greatly humbled, even to the death. His offices of Prophet, Priest, and King were treated with corruption along with himself. How great a position he held!

Seventh, did the sins you committed during a particular time, or before certain witnesses, cause the sin to become more heinous? Consider how God ordained to have the shame and affliction of his Son's death magnified by all these circumstances. It was a most accursed death, at a most solemn time, in a most infamous place, with the most wretched company.

So, may we discover that in Christ's suffering and propitiation, he has adequately answered anything our sins may have against us, and we should, therefore, be abundantly relieved. May our hearts and consciences be distinctly and particularly satisfied in the all-sufficiency of worth and merit which is found in the satisfaction Christ has made. In the same way that it is a fault and defect in humiliation when men become content with a general apprehension and notion that they are sinners, and yet never become genuinely humbled, so too is it a defect in their faith when they become content with a superficial and general pride that Christ died for sinners, yet their hearts are not particularly satisfied by the transcendent all-sufficiency of his death. Just as God was satisfied in Christ's death, so you should endeavor, by faith, to see the worth of Christ's satisfaction of God that your faith will rest in him and be satisfied as well.

""O death, where is your victory?" "O death, where is your sting?" The sting of death is sin, and the power of sin is the law. But thanks be to God, who gives us the victory through our Lord Jesus Christ."

1 CORINTHIANS 15:55-57

THREE

Confidence in Christ's Resurrection

The Resurrection Satisfies Faith
Christ as the Evidence of Our Justification

Although Christ's obedience in his life and his death merit all that is needed for our justification, the resurrection more fully satisfies our faith by seeing that God is satisfied and the payment for our sins has been accepted. With the resurrection as our evidence, our faith may come boldly to God. This is why the apostle Paul can cry victory over sin, hell, and death as the conclusion to the large discourse about Christ's resurrection in 1 Corinthians 15:55–57, "'O death, where is your victory? O death, where is your sting?' The sting of death is sin, and the power of sin is the law. But thanks be to God, who gives us the victory through our Lord Jesus Christ."

Christ as the Influence of Our Justification
But surely this is not all, as if our justification should only be argued by way of evidence. This alone would not have deserved such an emphasis if Christ's resurrection did not have some effective influence into our justification. Therefore, although the material cause of our justification is the obedient life and sacrificial death of Christ, the act of pronouncing us righteous also depends upon Christ's resurrection. As Paul says in 1 Corinthians 15:17, "If Christ has not been raised, your faith is futile and you are still in your sins." In other words, although you could suppose faith to be produced in you upon the merit of Christ's dying, yet it would be in vain if Christ had not risen again, because your claim to justification itself would be void. This is said, because his resurrection was the way in which our sins were removed and acquitted, as stated in Romans 4:25, "He was delivered up for our trespasses and raised for our justification."

Therefore, while the laying down of Christ's life, and dying the death we deserved to die, was the price and satisfaction for our sins, it is the resurrection by which God justifies us and pardons us from our sins. In a word, two things are necessary in order to free a debtor and fully pardon their debt: 1) The payment of the debt 2) The tearing or canceling of the bond, or receiving a release in order to free the debtor. In this case, payment was provided by Christ's death, and the release to free from the death was provided by his resurrection.

The Resurrection Supports Faith
Christ as the Surety of Our Justification
It is important to consider how Christ sustained a double relation regarding our justification: 1) As the surety bound to pay the debt for us and to save our souls 2) As the common person, or as an attorney at law in our place. Both of these will show how the resurrection supports our faith, by way of evidence that the debt is paid and by way of influence that we are acquitted and cannot be condemned. Beginning with the former, a surety is one that accepts responsibility and is bound to do a thing for another, as to pay a debt for him, or to bring him safely to a certain destination. Once the surety has fulfilled his responsibility, then the party for whom he was acting has all obligations satisfied as well.

Christ as the Person of Our Justification
By our law, an attorney appears for another, and money received by him is reckoned as received by him to whom it is due. Likewise, ambassadors for princes represent their masters—what is done to them is reckoned as done to the prince, and their actions of of representation are as if the prince had accomplished it himself. Therefore, attorneys and ambassadors are distinct from a surety. A surety sets out to pay a debt for another, but a common person serves

to perform any common act, which by the law is reckoned and virtually imputed to another. God has ordained Christ to be both a surety for us and also a common person representing us and acting in our place, as of a Husband, Head, Father, Brother, King, Priest, and Captain so that the fullness of his love might be extended to us. In this way, we are legally and formally justified and are assured that we will never be condemned.

The Resurrection Secures Faith
Christ as the Guarantee of Our Justification
Concerning the resurrection's provision for our faith, Christ was appointed and took on the task of being our guarantee. We see this in Hebrews 7:22, "This makes Jesus the guarantor of a better covenant." In every way, Christ became a guarantee to God for us, both to pay our debt by experiencing death in our place to satisfy God and then as the heir to execute his will and testament. He became a guarantee of the entire New Covenant, and every condition in it, both on God's part and on ours.

For us, Christ set out to actively obey God in every way, to receive all of our punishment, to pay our debts, and to work in us all that God requires of us. Therefore, to be a guarantee is much more than simply an intercessor or mediator. God said to Christ, as it were, "What they owe me, I require it all at your hands." Christ agreed, and from eternity shook hands with God to do everything for us that God could require and took on the penalty that we deserved.

Yes, Christ became a perfect guarantee for us. In fact, God has made the covenant of grace primarily with Christ, for us. His single oath alone was accepted for all so that God might be completely satisfied. Therefore he laid all upon Christ, committing not to deal with us, or so much as expect any payment from us, all according to his grace. We see an example of this in Psalm 89:19, where the mercies of the covenant made between Christ and God, under the type of God's covenant with David, are set forth, "Of old you spoke in a vision to your godly one, and said: 'I have granted help to one who is mighty.'" It's as if God had said, "I know that these will fail me, and break, and never be able to satisfy me, but you are a mighty and substantial person, able to pay me, and I will look for my debt from you." In this way, God has engaged himself to require satisfaction at Christ's hands, who is our guarantee.

Christ as the Promise of Our Justification
No news could be more welcome to sinners than to have a certain and infallible promise that we have been acquitted completely to God's satisfaction. The evidence for this promise lies in the resurrection: "Christ is risen" (Luke 24:34). Therefore, the debt has certainly been cleared, Christ has paid it in full, he is now without sin, and has been fully vindicated. God arrested Christ, as it were, cast

him into prison, began a trial against him to be judged, and he could not come out until he paid every last penalty. The strength of sin, God's wrath, and the curse against sin held him like cords. Christ could not have broken through this for the wrath of the all-powerful God was this prison, from which there was no escaping and no bail. Nothing would be accepted to let him go free but full satisfaction.

Therefore, to hear that Christ is risen and has come out of the prison is evidence of the promise that God is satisfied. Christ has been discharged by God himself. Because of this, the apostle Paul proclaims a mighty victory, obtained by Christ's resurrection, over death, the grave, the strength of sin, and the law. He cries out, "Thanks be to God, who gives us the victory through our Lord Jesus Christ" (1 Cor. 15:55–57). For this reason, you may now rest secure indeed: "Christ is risen; who is to condemn?" (Rom. 8:34).

The Resurrection Sustains Faith
Christ as the Representative of Our Justification
Now, if you ask in what way Christ was a common person, representing us, and standing in our place, I answer: he represented us in everything, in all conditions and states, and in what he experienced here on earth, in particular. For he had no other purpose to come down into this world, but to sustain us, to act in our place, and to have what should have been done to us, done to him.

This is why the apostle Paul, in 1 Corinthians, argues Christ to be a common person in respect to his condition and state through an argument which parallels his type, Adam (1 Cor. 15:45–49). In Romans 5, he speaks of Adam as a common person, both in respect of what he did, namely, his sin, and also in respect to the consequence of his sin, namely, death and condemnation. Adam was not merely considered a single man, but as a representative of all men. Therefore, both what he did and the condemnation and death deserved by his sin falls upon all.

Here, then, is where the matter stands regarding our justification and salvation between Christ and elect believers, for Adam was his type. Christ was considered and appointed by God as a common person, both in what he did and in what was done to him.

So according to the same law, what Christ did for us is reckoned or imputed to us, as if we ourselves had done it. And, what was done to him, tending to our justification and salvation, is reckoned as done to us. Therefore, when Christ died, he died as a common person, and God reckons that we died also.

When Christ arose, he rose as our head, and as a common person, and God accounts that we rose with him as well. It is by virtue of that communion which we have with him in all those actions, that we are now born again. Through the power of his resurrection, we do rise from both the guilt of sin and from the power of it.

Christ as the Perfector of Our Justification

In God reckoning us dying with Christ, then, we should reckon ourselves the same. As the apostle Paul says in Romans 6:10–11, "For the death he died he died to sin, once for all, but the life he lives he lives to God. So you also must consider yourselves dead to sin and alive to God in Christ Jesus." So although we are not yet completely "dead to sin" nor perfectly "alive to God," it is through "Jesus Christ," our Lord and representative, that we should "consider ourselves dead." And in this way, the apostle suggests to our faith the greatest encouragement: although our mortification of sin is imperfect, we may assure ourselves that one day our sins will be perfectly dead by virtue of Christ.

Furthermore, this assurance is also the strongest argument and motivation for the mortification of our sins. We should think it the greatest absurdity in the world to sin, even the smallest of sins, since we died long ago with Christ: "How can we who died to sin still live in it?" (Rom. 6:2). Of course, it might be said, "Oh! We are but imperfectly dead; and only from an imperfect death could such an imperfect argument have been drawn." But the Scripture elsewhere tells us that Christ, by his death, has "perfected for all time those who are being sanctified" (Heb. 10:14), so also in his death we may reckon ourselves perfectly dead by faith, and perfectly sanctified, although the work is not actually and fully perfected.

Finally, just as Christ has represented us in his death,

he has also done so in his resurrection. In 1 Corinthians 15:20, the apostle Paul argues that elect believers must and will rise, because "Christ has been raised from the dead, the first fruits of those who have fallen asleep." So the emphasis of this argument is founded upon the notion and consideration that Christ was a common person representing all the rest. Therefore, when we are all dead, Christ as the first fruit rises, both in our name and place, and guarantees that we will rise with him and in him.

The Resurrection Seals Faith
Christ as the Vindicated Justifier of Our Justification
Since Christ was made sin for us, and satisfied the penalty of sins on our behalf, there must also be some pronouncement of acquittal of those sins, which fully clears him and formally justifies him in respect to those sins. It is evident that this kind of acquittal was given by God, because we read that Christ, while he lived, and also in his death, was offered to "bear the sins of many" (Heb. 9:28). Yet, we read in the same passage that Christ will appear without sin. So, the alteration or discharge of these sins must have been made by God, for he alone is the only one who can give the acquittal. I submit to you that this acquittal took place at Christ's resurrection.

We see evidence of this in 1 Timothy 3:16. After saying that Christ "was manifested in the flesh," the text says that the God–man was "vindicated by the Spirit." That is to say that God appeared in the flesh to condemn sin in the flesh, but the power of his Godhead and divine nature, through the Spirit, raised him from the grave. And, through that raising he was justified by God and declared justified by that resurrection.

Another proof of this is found in Psalm 16:9–10, "Therefore my heart is glad, and my whole being rejoices; my flesh also dwells secure. For you will not abandon my soul to Sheol, or let your holy one see corruption." Of course, in the book of Acts, Peter interprets these words to refer to Christ's resurrection on two different occasions. Christ had been declared condemned by his death, so to be justified is part of his resurrection. It was a declaration to the world that God had vindicated him of all the sins that were laid on him. Therefore, because he was brought back to life and raised by the power of the Godhead, it demonstrates that he was also justified by God, and declared justified by the resurrection.

So it is that our justifier has been justified, "Therefore, as one trespass led to condemnation for all men, so one act of righteousness leads to justification and life for all men" (Rom. 8:18). Just as Christ was our representative in his death, so too in his resurrection, as he was justified. When he died, "the righteous" was put to death "for the unrighteous" (1 Pet. 3:18), so when he arose and was justified, the just that needed no justification was justified for the unjust. Therefore, we have been justified with him, and our justification is made irrevocable forever.

The Resurrection Sanctions Faith
Christ as the Victor of Our Justification
It is here that the triumph of faith is grounded in Christ's resurrection, "Who is to condemn? Christ Jesus is the one…who was raised" (Rom. 8:34). The meaning of this is that Christ was justified at his resurrection, and we were justified in him. This act was a solemn discharge from all sin and condemnation. It was a legal acquittal given to Christ for all our sins. His death was the satisfaction and payment for our sins, but his resurrection was the pardon. In this way, our justification and atonement is like a copy fetched from the roll of the court sentence that was pronounced. And this act is irrevocable and irrepealable. If we were justified when Christ was raised and justified, then our justification cannot be reversed. Rather, it stands as legal and warrantable as any act that God or man has ever ratified or confirmed. So, who is to condemn?

Let there be no mistake. It is necessary that we be justified in our own experience by faith. This is how we lay hold upon what God did for us in Christ. For according to the revealed rules of his word, there is a curse and a sentence of condemnation pronounced against us, under which we stand until he shall remove it by giving us faith. Therefore, it is only when we first believe that justification is actually and personally applied to us. So, while at

Christ's resurrection the act and sentence of justification was virtually pronounced upon us, it necessarily requires, from God's hands, the bestowing of faith upon us. By virtue of Christ being raised from the dead, we come to actually be justified in our own consciences and before all the world.

To confirm that God accounts all the elect justified in his justifying of Christ, we don't have to go any further than the words of the apostle from Romans 8:34. This text is especially significant when we consider where they are originally found, namely in Isaiah 50:8, "He who vindicates me is near. Who will contend with me?" As the context shows, these words were spoken by Christ to comfort himself against the Jews' condemning him, knowing that God would bring him justification.

Make no mistake, those very words of Christ which come through Isaiah, are the same words Paul boldly applies in like triumph to all the elect of Christ, "Who shall bring any charge against God's elect? It is God who justifies" (Rom. 8:33). He says this because Christ has died, has risen, and has been acquitted by God. Christ spoke those words as a public person in the name of all his elect. He died and was condemned for them, and he was justified from that condemnation, and they in him. So, when Christ accomplished all of this in our place, we triumphed with him.

The Resurrection Sanctifies Faith
Christ as the Communion of Our Justification

We find a picture of our communion with Christ in his resurrection, both in respect of sanctification and justification, in baptism. The prominent thing signified and represented in baptism is not simply the blood of Christ as it washes us from sin. There is also another aspect represented as well. Those who are baptized are seen buried under water, and then rising out of it, and this is not mere conformity to Christ in his baptism, but a representation of a communion with Christ in his death and resurrection.

In both Romans 6:3–4 and Colossians 2:12, it is said that we are "buried with him in baptism." So baptism represents our communion and oneness with Christ in his resurrection. It signifies that Christ once carried all the persons of the elect in his burial and resurrection and now, that the person who is baptized, is personally, particularly, and apparently demonstrating his belonging to Christ. It demonstrates that his communion with Christ was present while Christ died, was buried, and rose again. Upon that ground, the outward sign of baptism is a representation that the person has been buried with Christ and rises again.

Furthermore, there is an inward effect found in this ordinance of baptism. 1 Peter 3:21 refers to it as "an appeal to God for a good conscience," which is ultimately attributed to Christ's resurrection, but is signified and represented

ASSURANCE

in baptism. To unpack these words, our conscience is the principle in us which is the seat of guilt for all our sins and the courtroom where all come who wish to accuse us. The conscience is referred to as either good or evil depending on the state of the man. If his sins remain unpardoned, then he is condemned, and his conscience is said to be evil. If his sins have been forgiven, and he has been justified, then his conscience is said to be good. So in baptism, forgiveness of sins and justification are sealed up, if you will, to a believer's faith and conscience, under that dramatic representation of his communion with Christ in his resurrection.

In conclusion, by way of application or direction to a believer's faith, it is important to know how to make use of Christ's resurrection in our lives. Since our sins are presently mortified imperfectly, when temptations arise, Scripture calls us to respond to them by faith. We are to consider ourselves completely dead to sin because Christ died, and we were with him, "How can we who died to sin still live in it?" (Rom. 6:2). So God would have our faith make use of our communion with Christ in his death as a means of sanctification. In doing so, when guilt of sin arises in your conscience to accuse or threaten condemnation, you will reason with yourself that you have been justified in Christ, in his justification, which took place at his resurrection. So, see that God would have you use your communion with Christ as an argument to move you to mortify sin.

And should your heart object and say, "But I know not whether I was one of those whom God numbered justified with Christ when he arose." Then go to God and ask him boldly, whether or not he did this for you, and whether or not you were one chosen by him. Put the question to God and God will, by the power of Christ's resurrection, increase your faith with his answer before you even realize it. He will not deny it. And to give you greater assurance, know that however Christ will choose to interact with you, causing your heart to be drawn to surrender itself to him, you will never be condemned.

"For I am sure that neither death nor life, nor angels nor rulers, nor things present nor things to come, nor powers, nor height nor depth, nor anything else in all creation, will be able to separate us from the love of God in Christ Jesus our Lord."

ROMANS 8:38-39

FOUR

Confidence in Christ's Ascension

Christ Triumphant in Power and Authority
The Strengthening of Our Faith

We come to the next great pillar and support of faith, Christ being at God's right hand. And to show how seeing and considering Christ ascended strengthens faith, which seeks justification and pardon from sin, we look to Romans 8:34, "Who is to condemn? Christ Jesus is the one—who is at the right hand of God, who indeed is interceding for us." Here, the resurrection of Christ, and his sitting at God's right hand, are brought in as the ground of this bold challenge and triumph of faith.

The words of the apostle Peter further confirm, "who has gone into heaven and is at the right hand of God, with angels, authorities, and powers having been subjected to him (1 Pet. 3:22). The soul, then, has sufficient answer against condemnation in Christ's death and resurrection, full enough that it should stop there. In those realities faith can triumph, because it can show that full satisfaction has been provided in his death, his acceptance by God for us, and Christ's vindication, with us in him. But then let our faith go on to consider Jesus sitting at God's right hand, and making intercession for us. In doing so, faith will triumph over all accusers and be more than a conqueror. "For if while we were enemies we were reconciled to God by the death of his Son, much more, now that we are reconciled, shall we be saved by his life" (Rom. 5:10). And the meaning is this: if Christ's death had the power to pay all our debts, and justify us initially, then much more does his life have this power. So, then, his death is but the ground and foundation of our faith, and the lowest step of this ladder, but these others are the top where full triumph of faith is found.

The Rising of Our Spirits
And, our spirits should rise, just as the apostle's does. Faith upon these wings may not only fly above the gunshot of all accusations and condemnations, but even completely out of their sight, and so far above all such thoughts and fears, as it may reach to a level of assurance that sins are forgotten and will be remembered no more. What will you say when you see your assurance ascended up to heaven "far

above all rule and authority and power and dominion?" (Eph. 1:21). Therefore, first view him as ascending into heaven before he ever comes to be at God's right hand, and see what level of triumph that will provide you. This is what the words of the apostle Peter, quoted above, intended to convey: 1) Christ's ascension and 2) his power and authority there. And therefore both are to be considered for faith's triumph and for our comfort.

Christ Exalted in Boldness and Blessing
The Blessing of Justification
Before leaving the earth and ascending into heaven, Christ blessed his disciples, leaving all the elect with a blessing upon the earth, to the end of the world (Luke 24:51). The true reason and purpose for this blessing to them was because he was now going to carry out the eternal office of his priesthood in heaven. In blessing them, it was as if Christ was saying, "Oh my brethren, I have been dead, and in dying made a curse for you. Now that curse I have fully removed, and my Father has acquitted me and you for it. And now I can be bold to bless you, and pronounce all your sins forgiven, and your souls justified." For that is the intention and foundation of blessing, "Blessed is the one whose transgression is forgiven, whose sin is covered" (Ps. 32:1). This is the true meaning of Christ blessing them, which he reserved as his final earthly act. It was to show how by his death that he had redeemed them from

the curse of the law, and now going to heaven, was able to bless them with "every spiritual blessing in the heavenly places," and which heaven can afford (Eph. 1:3).

So, just as in Abraham, blessed by Melchizedek, all the faithful were blessed, so in these apostles all the elect to come are blessed. And therefore he has blessed all who would believe in Christ through their word, to the end of the world (John 17:20). Like God completing his work of creation and blessing it, Jesus Christ looked and pronounced blessing upon his redemptive work, and then went to heaven to keep and enjoy the Sabbath of all there.

The Persuasion of Justification

Let us also see Christ ascending and see what comfort it will also provide to our faith, towards the persuasion of justification. The apostles stood gazing on him and so should we lift up our hearts to gaze on him by faith. Let us view him in that act, as he is passing along into heaven, leading sin, hell, death, and the devil in triumph, at his chariot wheels. And in doing so, let your faith triumph, in further evidence of justification. This is seen in Ephesians 4:8, which is quoted from Psalm 68:18, as the apostle Paul says, "When he ascended on high he led a host of captives." Christ led captive all our spiritual enemies that would have captivated us. Now, the leading of captives always takes place after a perfect victory. And therefore, while at his death he had conquered them, at his rising he scattered them, and now at his ascension he leads them captive. So, the psalmist begins, in Psalm 68:1, "God shall arise, his enemies shall be scattered; and those who hate him shall flee before him!" And at his resurrection they did. Then, he ascends in triumph as a token of victory, "he ascended on high" (Ps. 68:18). So, like David, Christ ascends up to Mount Zion.

In doing so, two triumphant acts are mentioned (Eph. 4:8). The first was in leading a host of captives. It was customary in Rome, after a great military victory, for the conqueror to go up to the Capitol, while leading the captives bound to his chariot wheels. This is what Christ has done when dealing with our sins and all his enemies.

The second triumphant act is distributing gifts. "He gave gifts to men." It was also the Roman custom, after a victory, to cast new coins among the multitude. In similar fashion, Christ hands out the greatest gifts for the good of men that have ever been given. Therefore, sins and devils are not only dead, but triumphed over. As Colossians 2:15 says, "He disarmed the rulers and authorities and put them to open shame, by triumphing over them in him."

But then, after defeating these enemies on the cross, he continued to make a triumphant, public spectacle of them in his own person. It was the practice of the Roman emperors, in their great victories, to ride through the city of the greatest state and have all the trophies of their victory in front of them. The kings and nobles, whom they had captured, would be tied to their chariots and led around as captives. This is what Christ has done in his ascension. He has plainly demonstrated, by this public show of them at his ascension, that he has completely defeated and fully subdued them on the cross. It was the law that if the Roman emperors or generals themselves took anything into war, they had a particular responsibility to showcase it in triumph. Now Christ conquered in himself, and therefore triumphed in himself, and himself alone. And therefore, it was our Redeemer who not only broke sin's bars, flung off the gates of hell, and came out of the prison he was in, but as a demonstration of his victory, took them on his back and carried them up the hill. Like Samson did with the gates of the city on a high hill, Christ carried them on his own shoulders. So, then, did Christ triumph? Then let your faith triumph also, for Christ accomplished this victory in your place. This is why the apostle Paul tell us that, "We are more than conquerors" (Rom. 8:37).

The Satisfaction of Justification

Next, we see Christ entering into heaven. When he comes first to court after this great accomplishment, how does God look on him? Is God satisfied with what he has done? As you know, when a general comes home, there is commonly a great number of observers gathering to see how the king looks upon his service, according to how he performed the commission he was given. Christ, as our guarantee, took on the mission for sinners to fully conquer all our enemies, and God looks upon him to indicate that he has done it perfectly.

So, behold, Christ is like a conqueror who has entered heaven. Let that convince you that he has satisfied the debt and accomplished his commission down to the letter. God would never have allowed him to return to heaven if he had not done so. Instead, as soon as he would have peeped into heaven, he would have sent him back down again to finish the mission. But God lets him enter in, he comes boldly and confidently, and God lets him stay there. Therefore, be convinced that he has given God full satisfaction.

Christ Enthroned in Confidence and Splendor

As soon as Christ was carried into heaven, one could look and see all the angels falling down and worshiping him, and his Father welcoming him, with the highest honor that has ever been shown. The words which he then spoke we have recorded in Psalm 110:1, "The Lord says to my Lord: 'Sit at my right hand, until I make your enemies your footstool.'" And what do you say? Are you satisfied yet that God is satisfied for your sins? What superabundant evidence must Christ sitting at God's right hand give to a doubting heart? It argues, first, that Christ, for his part, has perfectly done his work and that there is no more left for him to do by way of satisfaction. This is what the word *sitting* implies. Secondly, it argues that God is fully satisfied on his part. This is what the phrase *sitting at God's right* hand implies.

A Throne of Completion

For the first argument, the phrase sitting does not denote rest, as in when work is fulfilled and finished. Christ was not to return until he had accomplished his work. In Hebrews 10:11, the apostle compares the force and excellence of Christ's sacrifice, with those of the priests of the old law, saying, "every priest stands daily at his service, offering repeatedly the same sacrifices, which can never take away sins." Their standing implied that they could never make satisfaction, so as to say, "we have finished it." "But when Christ had offered for all time a single sacrifice for sins, he sat down at the right hand of God" (Heb. 10:12). Notice how he contrasts their standing with his sitting down. He sat down as one who had completed his work. Therefore, Hebrews 4:10 says, "for whoever has entered God's rest has also rested from his works as God did from his."

A Throne of Satisfaction

Secondly, Christ being seated at God's right hand strongly argues that God is satisfied. For if God had not been infinitely well pleased with Christ, he never would have let him come so near to him, much less have advanced him to the exalted position of his right hand. And therefore, this is manifest evidence that he offered up such a satisfactory sacrifice that it has pleased God forever. In doing so, he took his place at God's right hand as confirmation of it, possessing the highest place in the heavenly court.

Christ Crowned in Provision and Purpose

We've now seen what triumphing evidence and demonstration, both Christ's ascension and sitting at God's right hand, do provide for us. With Christ considered our guarantee, he has therefore undoubtedly subdued our enemies and sins, and satisfied God. Let us consider, further, what force, efficacy, and influence these aspects have in them towards providing assurance and accomplishment of the salvation of believers, his elect.

The Jewels of His Crown

Upholding our confidence further are two aspects of Christ ascending. The first is the great end and purpose of his ascension, which is the errand, or business he ascended to accomplish, which was to prepare a place for us so that we can make our way to him. This he assures his disciples in John 14:2, "In my Father's house are many rooms. If it were not so, would I have told you that I go to prepare a place for you?" Just as Joseph was secretly sent ahead by God's sovereign intention, to prepare a place in Egypt for his brethren, whom God's providence meant to bring after him, even more openly does Christ ascend to heaven, declaring his purpose to be preparing a place for us. Flowing from the glorious welcome Christ received upon entering heaven, it is as though Christ says to God: "I do not come alone. I have a multitude. I have many brethren and followers who will be coming after me, for whom I prayed when I was on the earth, that they, "may be with me where I am" (John 17:24). And now that I am here, my train must come in too, for I am not complete without them. If you receive me, you must receive them also, and I have come to prepare their eternal homes."

Therefore, the Captain of our salvation has been "crowned with glory and honor" (Ps. 8:5). He brings "many sons to glory" (Heb. 2:10). So Christ essentially says, "Behold, I am their Captain, and they must follow me. Where I am they must be. See! I am here, and I am not to come alone, but to bring to glory all the children which you have given me." In response, God will essentially say, "They are all welcome." There is room enough for them, "many rooms," so there is no need to fear, or to say in our hearts doubting and despairing, "Who will ascend into heaven" for us? (Rom. 10:6). Christ has done it.

The Names on His Breastplate

Christ entered into heaven in our very names. In doing so, "Jesus has gone as a forerunner on our behalf" (Heb. 6:20). A forerunner is a forerunner of followers. So in Hebrews 12:23, we find ourselves in, "the assembly of the firstborn who are enrolled in heaven." And in 1 Peter 1:4, we see that our inheritance is being, "kept in heaven for you." Therefore, in like manner to the high priest, who entered into the holy of holies, with all the names of the tribes on his breast, so too does Christ with ours. He does this for a greater purpose than simply to prepare a place for us. It is to take possession of a place and give us a right to be there.

So through this consideration, may your faith see yourself as good as in heaven already, for Christ has entered in for you. Justification has two parts: first, acquittal from sin and freedom from condemnation, which gives ownership to eternal life. Now dying and rising as a common person for us, acquires the first, and it sets us perfectly enough in that state of freedom from condemnation. But then, this Christ, entering into heaven as a common person, sets us far above that state of non-condemnation. It places us in heaven with him. You would think of yourself secure if you had already ascended into heaven. Well, Christ has ascended and entered into heaven before you, so that when you die, you will go to heaven, to the place he has prepared.

Christ Seated in Sovereignty and Headship

As we consider Christ seated at the right hand of God, it should add more assurance to our faith. If we reflect upon either the power and authority of the position itself, and what it means to sit at God's right hand, or the relation Christ has with God as he sits there, both of these aspects combine to add strength in a mutually encouraging way.

Sovereignty of Power and Majesty

In Matthew 26:64, Jesus speaks of being "seated at the right hand of power." As we see in Ephesians 1:20–22, the privilege of God seating him at his right hand involves putting "all things under his feet." This phrase indicates the highest magnitude of sovereignty and power, which is not possessed by any creatures, angels, or men. And therefore, by that very phrase, the apostle argues in Hebrews 2 that that man of whom David had spoken in Psalm 8, was none other than Christ. It was not Adam, and not the angels, for neither of them has God subjected all things. And, to make his seat of authority more pronounced, God has made his footstool a world of enemies (Ps. 110), which is the highest triumph in the world.

Now, to what end has God committed this power to Christ? Is it not that he, himself, may be his own executor, and administrator, and perform all the inheritances which he provided to those for whom he died? As the expression is stated in Hebrews 9:15–17, so that none of his heirs might be wronged. There could never be fairer dealing or greater security given to us than this. The very purpose for which God invested Christ with this sovereign power is declared by Christ himself, "you have given him authority over all flesh, to give eternal life to all whom you have given him" (John 17:2). And, at his ascension, Christ was able to comfort his disciples in the fruit of their ministry.

In Matthew 28:18, he says, "All authority in heaven and on earth has been given to me." What holy confidence should this cultivate in us! He is at God's right hand, and we are in his hands (John 10:28). And, all his enemies are under his feet, so who can pull us out of his grasp? Christ declares, "I have the keys of Death and Hades" (Rev. 1:18). So, Christ has both the keys of death, the side gate out of this world and of hell, and even of the broad gates of that eternal prison. Therefore, not one of his sheep can be retrieved out of this world by death, unless Christ first opens the door, and they certainly cannot go to hell without his permission. Because of his resurrection, we may see and rest assured that he has the keys of death and hell, and by his ascension and position at God's right hand, we may recognize and be confident that he has the keys of heaven, whose door he has unlocked and now sits open. Why do we need to fear hell when Christ, our Redeemer, has the keys to it?

Sovereignty of Authority and Judgment
In addition, to sit at God's right hand entrusts all judgment to be committed to him, for sitting was a posture of judges. As Christ declared in John 5:21–22, "the Son gives life to whom he will. For the Father judges no one, but has given all judgment to the Son." Now, if he who loved us so, and died for us, is the Judge, himself, then, "Who is to

condemn?" (Rom. 8:34). Christ sits on God's right hand.

But Christ also sits down as the head to his people, as we see spelled out in Ephesians 1. In verse 21, the apostle speaks of power being advanced to God's right hand, "far above all rule and authority and power and dominion, and above every name that is named, not only in this age but also in the one to come." He goes on to declare how God has "put all things under his feet and gave him as head over all things to the church" (v. 22). Notice that he is said to sit over all things, not merely in his own pure, personal right, as his inheritance as the Son of God, but it says that he specifically sits over all as the head of the church. So we recognize, then, that our relationship with Christ is involved, and our right is included, in his exaltation and commission. He sits not only as a Son, but also as a head. Furthermore, he sits not merely as a head without a body, but with members who must be with him. As the apostle adds in verse 23, "which is his body, the fullness of him who fills all in all." So in that way Christ is not complete without all his members, and would leave heaven if anyone was missing. We are united to Christ, and since he has ascended, we are like sparks that fly up to him. He took our flesh and carried it into heaven and left us his Spirit on earth, as both instruments and deposits that we should follow him.

Yet, further still, Christ is not only said to be our head, but it is also said of us that he has, "seated us with him in the heavenly places in Christ Jesus" (Eph. 2:6). It's not that God's right hand is communicable to us, for that is for Christ and Christ alone. However, as he sits in heaven, it is indefinitely expressed that we will sit on his throne with him. In Revelation 3:21, the intention of this is explicitly expressed, "The one who conquers, I will grant him to sit with me on my throne, as I also conquered and sat down with my Father on his throne." So, there is a proportion clearly seen, though with an inequality. We sit on Christ's throne, but only he sits on his Father's throne. In other words, Christ alone sits at God's right hand, and we sit on Christ's right hand.

Providing to us an even greater comfort, this realization indicates that at the end of time we will sit with Christ on his judgment seat, to judge the world with him. Luke 22:30 says, "that you may eat and drink at my table in my kingdom and sit on thrones judging the twelve tribes of Israel." So this is the nature of our sitting with him, as it is specified in relation to judgment, and in proclaiming sentences, with not a sentence to pass without your votes.

So as an encouragement to your faith, don't just look at yourself as already being in heaven, and sitting with Christ, but look at yourself as a judge as well, so that if any sin should arise to accuse or condemn, it must be with your vote. What greater assurance can you have than this?

"Consequently, he is able to save to the uttermost those who draw near to God through him, since he always lives to make intercession for them."

HEBREWS 7:25

FIVE

Confidence in Christ's Intercession

An Introduction to His Intercession

We have seen Christ sitting at God's right hand as a judge and a king, having all authority of saving or condemning in his own hands. We have seen him having all power in heaven and earth to give eternal life to them that believe and the confidence that gives us. Let us now come to his intercession. The influence it has on our justification and salvation is like the last stroke of completion and is as great a stroke as any of the former. Just as you have read that there was an all-sufficiency in Christ's death—"Who is to condemn? Christ Jesus is the one who died," and in his resurrection, "more than that, who was raised," as well as in his ascension, "who is at the right hand of God," we will now see it in his intercession, "who indeed is interceding for us" (Rom. 8:34).

The apostle rises even higher in Hebrews 7:25, saying, "Consequently, he is able to save to the uttermost those who draw near to God through him, since he always lives to make intercession for them." So if you could suppose that there was anything lacking in the former works of Christ, in terms of what they accomplish for us, it is his intercession that can do it "to the uttermost." If money could purchase our salvation, Christ's death has done it, which he laid down as a price and an equivalent ransom. If power and authority could affect it, Christ being seated at God's right hand, entrusted with all power in heaven and earth, will be applied to accomplish it. If favor and petitions added to these were necessary, Christ will use these as well as he forever makes intercession. We can be sure that whatever is needed to bring about our salvation, Christ will do it, and we will be saved.

The Excellence of His Intercession
High Priests as a Type of Christ
To begin, the role of intercession is one part of Christ's priesthood. His sitting at God's right hand is not only as a king armed with power and authority to save us, but also as a priest. As Hebrews 8:1 says, "we have such a high priest, one who is seated at the right hand of the throne of the Majesty in heaven." In the old Levitical priesthood, the high priest's office had two parts, both which harmonize

within the role. The first part is offering the sacrifice. The second part is presenting the sacrifice in the holy of holies, with prayer and intercession to God, petitioning him to accept it for the sins of the people. The first part was done outside, but the second was done within the holy of holies. You see this spelled out in many places, especially Leviticus 16, which provides the law about the high priest entering into the holy of holies. He was not to enter into the holy place until he had first offered a sacrifice for himself and the people.

Secondly, when he had killed the sacrifice, he was to enter into the holy of holies with its blood, sprinkle the mercy seat found within, burn incense, and cause a cloud to arise over the mercy seat. We also see this in Hebrews 13:11, where it says that, "the bodies of those animals whose blood is brought into the holy places by the high priest as a sacrifice for sin are burned outside the camp." So, both of these acts were instrumental to the role of high priesthood for atonement.

This role was accomplished as a type of Christ and his priestly office. This is why Hebrews 9:23 calls all those transactions under the ceremonial law, "copies of the true things," which are actually found in heaven. As it says, "For Christ has entered, not into holy places made with hands, which are copies of the true things, but into heaven itself, now to appear in the presence of God on our behalf" (Heb. 9:23).

The Ultimate High Priest

Therefore, in answer to this type, there are also two distinct parts of Christ's priesthood.

First, there was the sacrifice. Christ "put away sin by the sacrifice of himself" (Heb. 9:26). This corresponds to the killing of the sacrifice on the outside of the holy of holies, as Christ was crucified outside the city (Heb. 13:12)

Second, Christ carried his blood into the holy of holies, namely, the heavens (Heb. 9:12). There he appears, in Hebrews 9:24, to pray. The type of those prayers was that cloud of incense made by the high priest, as we learn from Revelation 8:3, that there "was given much incense to offer with the prayers of all the saints on the golden altar before the throne." This incense is Christ's own prayers in heaven, which he continually puts forward when the saints pray on earth, and so perfumes all their prayers, and obtains all blessings for them.

These parts of his priesthood are mentioned by the apostle John in 1 John 2:2, where he refers to Jesus Christ as "the propitiation for our sins." Likewise, he calls him our advocate in the previous verse, with both parts combining to fulfill this office. In addition, this work of intercession and bringing his blood into the holy of holies is actually an action he began on earth. The blood which he offered with tears and strong cries on the cross, where he also interceded, is the same blood he continues to essentially offer up with prayers in the heavens, and makes atonement by both, only with this difference: on earth, though he interceded, he primarily was offering up himself, while in heaven, though he entered with his offering, he now primarily intercedes.

The Perfection of His Priesthood

Christ's intercession in heaven was such a necessary part of his priesthood, that without it he would not have been a complete priest. As Hebrews 8:4 says, "Now if he were on earth, he would not be a priest at all." In other words, if he would have remained on earth, he would not have been a complete priest. Since the work of intercession still needed to be accomplished, if he would have remained on earth, it would have left his office imperfect. But Christ has ascended and now intercedes in the perfection of his priesthood.

The perfection of Christ's priesthood was typified by two figures who came before him, Aaron and Melchizedek. Beginning with Aaron, the highest service of his office was going into the holy of holies and making atonement there. This was the height of the priest's honor, which he did alone, and it was the primary thing which separated him, as high priest, from the other priests. The other priests offered daily sacrifices in the court of the priests, but only the high priest offered a sacrifice in the holy of holies every year. This was the high and transcendent privilege of the high priest. Comparatively, Christ, as high priest, entered into the heavens by his blood, sat down on the majesty on high, and through his sacrifice, now intercedes. In other words, in ultimate fulfillment of that priesthood, Hebrews 4:14 says, "Therefore, since we have a great high priest who has passed through the heavens, Jesus the Son of God, let us hold fast our confession."

The second figure typifying Christ was Melchizedek. We observe Psalm 110:4, which says of Christ, "You are a priest forever after the order of Melchizedek." From this verse, the author of Hebrews argues that his priesthood is much more excellent than Aaron's. Yet, from the transcendent excellency of Christ's priesthood, the most excellent part is that Christ, unlike Melchizedek, forever acts in heaven. Furthermore, "Christ has obtained a ministry that is as much more excellent than the old as the covenant he mediates is better, since it is enacted on better promises" (Heb. 8:6). The consummation of this perfect ministry was found in the presenting of his sacrifice in heaven and in his intercession.

The Purpose of His Intercession
That God Be Glorified
In general, God will interact with us in our salvation while keeping a distance between himself and sinners until the day of our glorification. And therefore, through Christ, we have a priest and a mediator to intercede on our behalf. God has set him up, as it were, as "King upon his holy hill"

(Ps. 2:6). Namely, this hill is in heaven, and he has committed all power in heaven and earth to him.

More particularly, God has two attributes which he desires to be most emphatically exalted in their highest glory by Christ accomplishing our salvation, namely, justice and free grace. And therefore, he has ordered the bringing about of salvation to occur in such a way that Christ will satisfy one and petition for the other. Justice will be known to be justice and dealt with on its own terms. Likewise, grace will be acknowledged to be free grace throughout the accomplishment of our salvation. You have both of these joined together in Romans 3:24, 26, which says that we are "justified by his grace as a gift, through the redemption that is in Christ Jesus…so that he might be just and the justifier of the one who has faith in Jesus." Here is the highest justice and the freest grace both meeting to save us, and both ordained by God to be declared and emphasized.

It was therefore imperative that, in Christ's priesthood, he should apply himself to both justice and free grace. Accordingly, in his death he deals with justice, by laying down a sufficient price. And in his intercession, he petitions free grace, and both are therefore emphasized. In Hebrews 4:16, it says, "Let us then with confidence draw near to the throne of grace," because "we have a great high priest who has passed through the heavens" (Heb. 4:14). Observe how it is called a throne of grace, which is where our high priest, who is now in heaven, presides. Because our high priest deals there primarily with free grace, it is called the throne of grace, as he interacts with God by way of intercession.

That His People Be Sanctified
Another reason God ordained Christ's intercession to be joined to his death was to bring about the completion of salvation and the assurance of our hearts. God's desire is for our salvation to be made certain. The first way he does that is through ransom and price, as captives are redeemed. This was accomplished through the death of Christ. The second way he does it is through power and rescue, which has been accomplished in the resurrection, ascension, and sitting at God's right hand. And finally, God makes our salvation certain by intercession, as Christ petitions for grace. These three are like a threefold cord, with each strong enough on its own, but all together will definitely hold.

Intercession, in particular, has a unique role in God's plan of redemption. There is a special dependence placed upon it in the application of our salvation. Christ purchased salvation by his death, but he assures that we will possess it by his intercession. Certainly, the resurrection has an influence on our justification, as we have previously noted, but it is much more proper to ascribe the application of our justification to his work of intercession.

One primary instance to show that Christ's intercession was to be the applying cause of salvation was given by Christ while he was on the earth, which gives us an illustration of the work that would be done by him in heaven. When he was on the cross and was offering himself as that great sacrifice for sin, he also, at that time, offered prayers for those that crucified him, "Father, forgive them, for they know not what they do" (Luke 23:34). This fulfilled the words of Isaiah 53:12, "yet he bore the sin of many, and makes intercession for the transgressors." And the efficacy of that prayer was the cause of the conversion of those three thousand in Acts 2:23, whom the apostle had expressly charged with crucifying Christ, saying, "this Jesus…you crucified and killed by the hands of lawless men." These were the first fruits of Christ's intercession, whose prayers still reap and bring in the rest of the crop, which is to grow up into God on earth until the end of the world.

We, ourselves, are included in the progress of Christ's intercession as well. Our initial justification, which was given to us at our conversion depends upon Christ's prayers. The very thing he prayed for on the cross was our forgiveness, "Father, forgive them" (Luke 23:34). This prayer is brought to fruition when our personal and actual justification occurs, which takes place when we believe (Rom. 5:1). And this depends upon Christ's intercession, which was typified by Moses sprinkling the people with

ASSURANCE

blood, referenced in Hebrews 9:19. This is the thing Jesus Christ as Mediator and Priest does now from heaven. For in Hebrews 12:24, it says that we have come to "Jesus, the mediator of a new covenant, and to the sprinkled blood." He shed his blood on the cross while on earth, but he sprinkles it now as a priest from heaven.

The continuation of our justification also depends upon Christ's work of intercession. Just as his intercession is the essential continuation of his sacrifice, it is also the continuing cause of our justification. Although it is a single act, yet it is renewed every moment, for it is continued by acts of free grace. Therefore, we owe our standing in grace every moment to his sitting in heaven and interceding every moment. There is no fresh act of justification that goes forward, but there is a fresh act of intercession.

Christ's position also provides full assurance that our justification will be remembered forever. And to that end, God has placed Christ as his remembrance for us, so near him that it would bring his thoughts to Christ's obedience so that our sins might not come into his mind. It is not as though God needed this help, but only as a demonstration that our fears would be calmed, our guilt would be silenced, and our faith would be strengthened. As an example, this is why God has ordained the rainbow in the heavens, that when he looks upon it, he might remember his covenant never to destroy the world by water again. Likewise, he has set Christ as the rainbow about his throne. We can also look to the bread and wine in the Lord's supper, which are appointed on earth to "proclaim the Lord's death until he comes" (1 Cor. 11:26). In like manner, Christ himself has been appointed in heaven to demonstrate his death as a remembrance to his Father.

That Christ Be Magnified

A final reason that God has ordained this work of intercession to accomplish our salvation, is so that Christ will be honored and glorified perpetually in our hearts. His great desire in the ordering of our salvation has been "that all may honor the Son, just as they honor the Father" (John 5:23). Therefore, for the maintaining and upholding of Christ's glory, after all that he accomplished on earth, God has ordained the work of intercession in heaven to be added to the rest, for the perfecting of salvation.

Furthermore, while all the persons of the Trinity have an equal hand in the work of our salvation, God's desire was for Christ to have a part in every aspect of our salvation, from first to last, in every step and degree of accomplishing it. This is expressed in Hebrews 12:2, as it refers to Jesus as, "the author and perfecter of our faith." These two particular aspects of authoring and perfecting should both be considered. First, we see it in his dying and "enduring the cross," as the verse goes on to say. This dying is "the beginning of our faith." But second, as we look to him sitting at God's right hand as intercessor, we find him "finishing our faith." In this way, Christ is, "the Alpha and the Omega, the first and the last, the beginning and the end" (Rev. 22:13).

So, as we look upon our Mediator, Christ, may we see him doing as much work for us in heaven, at this instant, as he ever did on earth. Here, he suffered, but there he is praying and presenting his sufferings. All his work was not done when he had finished here, but his work in heaven, though sweeter by far, yet lies on his hands forever. So, let us not ignore these aspects in our believing upon him.

The Security of His Intercession

We come at this point to show what solid grounds of security and triumph our faith may use to increase through Christ's intercession, and there are two primary demonstrations that act as evidence for us in this way. The first is the scope and purpose of the work of intercession itself. The second pertains to the intentionality of Christ on our behalf.

Comforting Our Souls

Now the perfection of every one of Christ's works lies in the purpose for which it was ordained. The immediate and direct end of Christ's intercession is the actual salvation of elect believers, which are the people for whom Christ died. The end of his death is a right to salvation, but the end of his intercession is actually the act of saving and putting us in possession of heaven. Observe how the Scripture speaks concerning Christ's death in Hebrews 9:12, "he entered once for all into the holy places…by means of his own blood, thus securing an eternal redemption." Romans 5:9–10 also speaks of this, saying, "having now been justified by his blood, we shall be saved from the wrath of God through him. For if while we were enemies we were reconciled to God through the death of his Son, much more, having been reconciled, we shall be saved by his life." This is Christ living to intercede so that the very salvation of believers is found in the work of Christ's intercession.

So what kind of security does this provide for us? To be saved is more than to be justified, for it is the actual possessing of heaven. So, then, we must grant that Christ's intercession is as perfect a work as Christ's death. Our sins are the object of one, and our souls are the object of the other. The comfort of our souls, then, is found in the perfection of his intercession.

You may respond, "my unfaithfulness and stubbornness may hinder it." To that, we reply that intercession takes on the work completely, for Christ doesn't pray conditional prayers in heaven saying, "If men will believe," as we do here on earth. Christ does not intercede merely for propositions, but for persons. And, therefore, Christ prays to cure that very unfaithfulness. He considers who we are, the condition of our souls, and what unbelief may be found in us, and he sets out to save us. This is the scope and purpose of his work. So, then, our comfort is this: Christ himself is a perfect priest, so we who come to God by him must be perfectly saved. For example, the work of his kingly office is to subdue all enemies, to the very last man. If he were to leave one enemy unsubdued, he would fail to be a perfect king. So it is with his priestly office. If only one soul of the elect, or those he interceded for, were left unsaved, he would fail to be a perfect priest. This is certainly the highest means of comfort for our souls.

Maintaining His Honor
Besides the nature and scope of Christ's work of intercession, as it provides us with comfort, there is an additional aspect of our security, and that is Christ's own honor. It is not the loss of a business that concerns him, or the loss of work, but it his own person that would be lost, if he were to fail in his role as intercessor. The book of Hebrews gives Christ the title of guarantor. And, although it holds true for all parts of his office, the concept of being a guarantor has a greater and more significant application to his role of intercession. Hebrews 7:22 says, "This makes Jesus the guarantor of a better covenant." And this is in reference to the office of priest, which is his forever. Therefore, Hebrews 7:25 concludes by saying, "Consequently, he is able to save to the uttermost those who draw near to God through him, since he always lives to make intercession

for them." Christ is a guarantor on earth, and is a guarantor in heaven, only with this double difference: that on earth he was a guarantor to pay a price so sufficient that it satisfied God's justice, but in heaven he remains a guarantor, bound by another obligation just as great, which is the bringing to salvation those for whom he died.

Therefore, we can recognize the difference in these guarantor roles by the differing aspects of honor Christ was at risk to forfeit. The first was the payment for our sin debt, with his soul itself at stake, which he offered up for sin. The second is in saving all the persons for whom he died, and in that his honor in heaven is at stake. So Christ lives to intercede. He possesses heaven upon these terms, and if he fails to bring us with him, he, himself, would have to quit heaven. May the consideration of this assure us in our faith all the more. For, the more honor that lies at stake, the more Christ will seek to accomplish it.

The Greatness of His Intercession

Now that we have heard the evidence that supports our faith, let us consider what further assurance will increase our faith, as it specifically pertains to the relationship Christ has with God, the one the Son, the other the Father. Together, we see the greatness of Christ with God and the graciousness of God to Christ, united in will and affection, so that Christ will be sure to ask nothing which the Father will deny, and his Father will not deny anything he will ask.

The Greatness of Christ with God
Now first, let us begin with the greatness of Christ the Intercessor, that is his greatness with God the Father. This is often encouraged in the epistle to the Hebrews, in order to create confidence in us, "Since then we have a great high priest…Let us then with confidence draw near to the throne of grace" (Heb. 4:14, 16). While great and priest are joined together, the more comfort and boldness we may have, the greater he is, for he is a priest in relation to his dealing with God for our pardon. As a priest, he deals with nothing else, and the greater the person is who applies himself accordingly, the better, for the sooner he will prevail. He is said to be great there, because he is great in prevailing with God, with such a greatness that it is impossible for him not to prevail.

It is the greatness of his person which provides such an influence through his death that it was a price more than enough to satisfy justice. And therefore, "Who shall condemn? It is Christ that died" (Rom. 8:34). And the greatness of his person must have as much influence to make intercession as he did in his death. In that way, Christ must necessarily be great with God in many respects.

The first way we see is in respect to the nearness of his alliance to him. Christ is the natural Son of God, God of God, and therefore certain to succeed with him.

Our Confidence in Christ

Intercession is a carrying on our salvation in a way of grace and favor, as his death was by way of satisfaction. It may be observed in Scripture that the all-sufficient satisfaction of his death is still present with him as God and connected to the greatness of his person in nature and essence, namely, his Godhead. In like manner, the frequency of his intercession is founded upon the nearness of his relation to God, his alliance with him, and the position of being his Son. Therefore, Christ not only intercedes according to the virtue and strength of his satisfaction, and from his obedience to his Father, but also in the strength of his relation to the Father, as his Son, who pleads his own grace and significance in God, which is a reality that always exists and abides.

So, while it could be supposed that Christ's obedience, because it happened so long ago, might be forgotten, the fact that he is a Son makes that an impossibility. And, how effectual must the intercession of such a Son be, who is so great a Son of so great a Father, equal with him and the express image of his person? Never has there ever been a Son like him, and in such a distinctly transcendent manner, as the relation of sonship among men is but a shadow of it! Christ is one with his Father, as he often speaks, and therefore, if his Father should deny him anything, he should then cease to be one with him, and he must deny himself, which God can never do. So as God himself is perfect and his power irresistible, so his priesthood through this relation might be perfect also, and his requests undeniable.

The Goodness of God to Christ
Christ intercedes not only as a Son, but also as a Son who has been obedient to his Father, serving at his request and for his sake. Christ has accomplished the greatest service for him and the most willingly that anyone has ever done. We see this in both his active and passive obedience. Beginning with his *active* obedience, Hebrews 7:26 describes Christ as, "such a high priest, holy, innocent, unstained, separated from sinners, and exalted above the heavens." Such a priest he was, and is therefore able to save by his intercession. For when requests come out of the lips of such a high priest, they must be accepted.

Then, the apostle also mentions Christ's *passive* obedience. In Hebrews 7:27, concerning his sacrificial death, he says, "he did this once for all when he offered up himself." And through that obedience, he made full satisfaction. So we see the value of justice in Christ's obedience to his Father, but we also see the goodness of God upon Christ's life. So transcendent was the obedience of Christ to his Father, as we see in Christ giving himself to death at his request, that he can never out-ask God.

Therefore, as a great encouragement to us, Christ has nothing left to ask for himself, for he has no need of anything. All his favor remains complete, which can be laid before sinners, and petitioned on their behalf. When we add to that the fact that anything Christ could ask on behalf of sinners is far less than the service which he has completed at his Father's request, we realize that our lives, our forgiveness, and our salvation are not enough to equal what Christ has done.

The Basis of His Intercession
Pleading for Justice
In addition to goodness and grace, Christ can and does plead for justice and righteousness. We see an example of this in 1 John 2:1–2, "we have an advocate with the Father, Jesus Christ the righteous. He is the propitiation for our sins, and not for ours only but also for the sins of the whole world." An advocate is only present when representing the cause of justice. And for Christ, as the Advocate, he pleads his own satisfaction. He appeals to his own righteousness to the point that justice itself will joyfully save the worst of sinners. As 1 John 1:9 says, "If we confess our sins, he is faithful and just to forgive us our sins and to cleanse us from all unrighteousness." He will take the worst case and make it a good one, not by coloring it over as cunning lawyers do, or by extenuating circumstances, but with pleading that righteousness, being put into the opposite balance, will be cast for you, and there can never be too many sins weighed against it.

While many things are said to cry in Scripture, blood

has the loudest cry of all things, in the ears of the Lord of Hosts, the Judge of all the world. Nothing has obtained the attention of God's justice more than that of blood. And, although Christ himself was silent, Hebrews 12:24 ascribes a voice of appeal and an intercession to the blood of Christ in heaven. "Jesus, the mediator of a new covenant, and to the sprinkled blood that speaks a better word than the blood of Abel." The reference to Abel's blood comes from Genesis 4:10, "And the Lord said, 'What have you done? The voice of your brother's blood is crying to me from the ground.'" Therefore, in contrast, Christ's blood calls for greater things to be bestowed on us for whom it was shed than Abel's blood did for evil things, and vengeance against Cain, by whom it was shed. Now to show the power of this cry from Christ's blood for justice, let us compare it with the cry of Abel's blood.

First, even the blood of the wickedest man on earth, if innocently shed, does cry and has a power with justice against the one who murdered him. Had Abel murdered Cain, Cain's blood would have cried and called upon God's justice against Abel. But Abel, who was a saint and the first martyr on God's calendar, had blood that cried out according to the worth that was in him. Now from this I argue, if the blood of a saint cries so, what must the blood of the King of saints then do? Oh, how it fills heaven and earth with outcries, until the promised intent of its shedding be accomplished! And look how the blood of Abel cried for the ruin and condemnation of his brother Cain. On the contrary, Christ's blood cries out so much louder for our pardon and justification.

Second, the cry of Christ's blood has a greater advantage than Abel's blood. For Abel's blood cried out from the earth, but Christ's blood has been carried up to heaven. For, as the high priest carried the blood of the sacrifices into the holy of holies, so has Christ carried, as it were, his blood into heaven. This blood, therefore, cries from heaven next to God who sits there as judge, and it cries in his very ears. Abel's blood cried for vengeance to come down from heaven, but Christ's blood cries us up into heaven.

Echoing the Cries
Furthermore, not only does the blood of Christ cry, but Christ himself being alive also joins his voice with it. Christ follows suit, echoing the cry of his own blood. And, his being alive puts life into his death. Why did God make a covenant with Abraham, Isaac, and Jacob, to remember their offspring after them? They were alive, and were to live forever, and though dead, shall rise again. So God reasons from that reality in Matthew 22:32, "I am the God of Abraham, and the God of Isaac, and the God of Jacob. He is not God of the dead, but of the living." So God remembers and respects his covenant with them, for he is a God of the living, and so his covenant holds with them while they live.

ASSURANCE

But this new covenant runs in the name of Christ, "The God and Father of our Lord Jesus Christ" (Eph. 1:3). And so he becomes our God and our Father in him. Since God becomes our Father, it works effectively for him to hear the cry of Christ's blood, and of Christ himself. To illustrate by the help of the former comparison, if Abel's blood cries, then it proves that Abel's soul lives to cry out for his cause. In other words, the cry of Abel's blood is seconded with the cry of Abel's soul that lives, doubly emphasizing the force of his plea. As we see in Revelation 6:9–10, it says that, "the souls of those who had been slain for the word of God and for the witness they had borne…cried out with a loud voice, 'O Sovereign Lord, holy and true, how long before you will judge and avenge our blood on those who dwell on the earth?'" Yes, see that not only does their blood cry, but their souls live, and live to cry as well.

Now not only does Christ's soul live to cry, but his whole person, for he is risen again, and lives to intercede forever. In Revelation 1:18, Christ appears to John, when he would give one speech, "I died, and behold I am alive forevermore." And his death was for you, so whose heart does not move to read his words with faith? And does it not move his Father, who was the chief cause and sovereign of his death, to think, "My Son that was dead and died at my request for sinners is now alive again, and lives to intercede?" "Who is to condemn? Christ Jesus is the one who indeed is interceding for us" (Rom. 8:34).

The Privilege of His Intercession
His Sovereign Pleasure
A further demonstration of both Christ's greatness with God and his power to triumph for us is found in the reality that God has put all power into his hand to do whatever he chooses. He has made him his king to do what pleases him either in heaven, earth, or hell, and to do all that God himself ever means or desires to do. And certainly if his Father has been so gracious to him, as to bestow such high and absolute sovereignty on him, then surely his purpose was never to deny Christ any request that he should make. God has made Christ King and "has given all judgment to the Son" (John 5:22). This means that he has given Christ the power even to save and condemn whomever he chooses.

Now then, if he who is king can do anything he chooses, and command anything he desires, as absolutely as God does, what will not be done? And, this same Christ is there at God's right hand to intercede. He treats the salvation of sinners as a mighty prince treats the giving up of some town to him, which lies seated under a castle of his, which commands that town. He stands discussing with the governor, prepared to advance the battery, and bring all into subjection.

His Generous Father
Now when the Father had first made and constituted

Christ as a great King, and had given him absolute power to command, he still instructed him to ask. It's as if the Father said, "Ask of me, and I will give you the ends of the earth for your inheritance. I cannot deny you, but I would have you ask, and therefore Christ asks." These are the terms between the Father and the Son. Therefore, if he who has so much power will join the power of petition with a Father who so loves him, and if he who is the word of his Father, that commands, creates, and upholds all, will ask all that he desires to do, how powerful his words will be!

Therefore, observe Christ's manner of praying in John 17:24, "Father, I desire that they also, whom you have given me, may be with me where I am." He prays like a king, who is in joint commission with God. If God puts that honor upon our prayers, then how much more does Jesus Christ's intercession command all in heaven and earth! Christ's Father will not displease him, nor go against him in anything.

Know that this Father and this Son, though two persons, have yet but one will between them, and but one power between them. "The Son can do nothing of his own accord, but only what he sees the Father doing. For whatever the Father does, that the Son does likewise" (John 5:19). They plan as one, have one power, one will. Therefore, it is no surprise that God has committed all power to the Son, and that the Son, though he has all power, must ask all of the Father. To be sure, whatever the Son asks, the Father will not deny, because they have one will and power.

The Grace of His Intercession
An Advocate with the Father

We have seen the greatness of the person interceding, and many considerations from there, which may persuade us of his triumph for us. Let us now consider the graciousness of the person with whom he intercedes, which the Scripture, for our comfort, distinctly sets before us. In doing so, the end of this vital matter is for our joy and security, that our every way may be abundantly blessed. This is why we see, in 1 John 2:1, for the comfort and support of believers against the evil of the greatest sins that can overtake them after conversion, the apostle reminding them of Christ's intercession by saying, "But if anyone does sin, we have an advocate with the Father, Jesus Christ the righteous." Certainly, mentioning the power and prevalence of such an advocate, according to his own righteousness, is vital. Yet, over and above this, in order to more fully assure us, he adds, "An advocate with the Father." In other words, he insinuates and suggests the relation and gracious character of him upon whose supreme will our case ultimately depends, "the Father."

Notice that he does not say, "an Advocate with *his* Father," though that would have given much assurance, or "with *your* Father," though that might produce much boldness. But indefinitely he says, "with *the* Father," as intending to take in both. You have both of these mentioned elsewhere more distinctly, intentionally, and together in John 20:17, "I am ascending to my Father and your Father," says Christ. And it was spoken after all his disciples had forsaken him, and Peter denied him, when Christ himself could send them the greatest words of affection his heart could utter, and wrap up the strongest transfer of comforts in one pill. What was it? Go, tell them, not so much that I have satisfied the penalty for sin, overcome death, or am risen, but that "I ascend." For in the work that Christ does for us in being ascended lies the height and the top of our comfort. And while he could have said "I ascend to heaven, and so, where I am you shall be also." Yet, he chooses rather to say, "I ascend to the Father," for that indeed contained the foundation, spring, and cause of their comfort, emphasizing his relationship to the Father, which Christ would engage in after his ascending for them. So, if Christ wanted to send good news from heaven to you, today, it would be this: "I am here, an advocate, interceding with my Father and your Father." Everything that needs to be said is spoken in that. Even the God of all comfort could not speak more comfort.

Interceding with the Father
Considering Christ's relationship to his Father, it should

provide us comfort and assurance to recognize that he intercedes with him. To confirm this, you have a double testimony from two of the greatest witnesses in heaven: the testimony of Christ, while he was on the earth, and God's own word also declared since Christ came to heaven. We see the first in John 11. When Lazarus had been dead for four days, Martha tells Christ that if he had been there before her brother died, then he would still be alive. Then, she adds, "But even now I know that whatever you ask from God, God will give you" (John 11:22). Here was her confidence in Christ's intercession, though this was a greater work than Christ, at that point, had ever done. And Christ, seeing her faith in this, confirmed her speech when he came to raise Lazarus, and took a solemn opportunity to declare that God has never denied him any request that he has ever petitioned, "Father, I thank you that you have heard me. I knew that you always hear me, but I said this on account of the people standing around, that they may believe that you sent me" (John 11:41–42). In other words, this is no new thing. Not just in this miracle, but in all miracles and in all requests, the Father hears the Son. Furthermore, the Son has never been denied by his Father and never will be.

Receiving from the Father
In addition, now that Christ has accomplished his earthly mission and has gone to heaven, we can see what the

Father plans to do for him. Statements like the one from Psalm 110:1, "Sit at my right hand, until I make your enemies your footstool" help us to see what the Father plans to do for his Son. And before Christ opened his mouth to speak a word, by way of making any request to God, the Father added, "You are my Son; today I have begotten you. Ask of me, and I will make the nations your heritage, and the ends of the earth your possession" (Ps. 2:7–8). In other words, it is as if the Father said, "I know you will ask me now for all you have died for, and this I promise you beforehand, before you speak a word, or make any request to me, it will be granted."

So full of joy was his Father's heart that he had his Son in heaven with him, whom he had begotten from everlasting, and ordained to this glory, who was, in a sense, dead, but was alive again. God's heart was so full that he could not keep from expressing it in the most magnificent favors and granting of requests. If human subjects can persuade earthly kings to grant their requests, then what will Christ, who is such a great Son, and even equal with his Father, not be able to succeed in obtaining from his Father for us? Regardless of how desperate our case may be, Christ can succeed in resolving them all.

The Power of His Intercession
The Inclination of the Father's Heart
How potent are the prayers of Christ for his people. This

is expressly stated in John 16:26–27, "In that day you will ask in my name, and I do not say to you that I will ask the Father on your behalf; for the Father himself loves you, because you have loved me and have believed that I came from God." That day, which Christ refers to, is the day when the Holy Spirit would be poured out upon them. And the scope of his intentions, here, is to convey the highest magnitude of promise that he will be praying for them, and to tell them where their more abundant assurance and security is found. Besides having the benefit of prayers, Christ wants them to know that God himself loves them from within himself. That alone is enough to obtain anything from his hands when they ask it in the name of Christ.

Now, as a contrasting parallel, to comfort his disciples, Christ says, "I do not say to you that I will ask the Father on your behalf." In other words, he's essentially saying, "I, who you will see die for you, if I spend my blood for you, will I not spend my breath for you? And yet, the truth is, though I will pray, I do not even need to, because 'the Father himself loves you.' How much more will you be saved, therefore, when I combine my prayers with his love for you?" Christ's intention was to let his disciples know that the inclination of his Father's heart is as much towards us, and for our salvation, as Christ's is. Furthermore, all that Christ does for us is but the expression of that love which originated in God's own heart. Therefore, it was out of that love that he gave Christ for us.

So, when we consider the love of God spoken of in John 3:16, we see that Christ's death was a means to demonstrate that love for us. Christ does not add one drop of love to God's heart. He only draws it out and makes it flow. The intercession of Christ, therefore, must be effective, as God's heart is prepared to flow toward us. When Christ speaks for us, and speaks God's own heart, how successful must those words be.

The Results of Christ's Work

Since Christ died for us, it assures us of the perfect price that was paid and the right to eternal life we have acquired.

Since Christ rose again in our place, this assures us even further that there is a formal, legal, and irrevocable act of justification passed and registered in the court of heaven between Christ and God, and that in Christ being justified, we have also been justified in him without the possibility of a recall.

Christ's ascension into heaven is a further act of his taking possession of heaven for us as he formally enters in our place, and this is further confirmed in our salvation. Yet, still in our own persons we are not saved, but only because we are representatively in Christ who is our head.

Since Christ now sits at God's right hand, he is armed and empowered with all power in heaven and earth to give and apply eternal life to us.

Since Christ now intercedes, he is working to finish and complete our salvation, even to save us. And, as Christ's death and resurrection were to establish our salvation, and by faith we receive it, our souls are not only sitting in heaven in Christ, but also through his intercession we actually belong to heaven.

All of these realities are possessed by faith, and I leave them with you to comfort your souls.

The Assurance of His Intercession
Concluding Words of Comfort
In conclusion, I will add a brief source of encouragement, especially for those who are the weakest in faith and who feel that they cannot obtain any sense of assurance, and are likewise discouraged in coming to Christ. And I will confine my words only to the most comforting words found in all of Scripture, "Consequently, he is able to save to the uttermost those who draw near to God through him, since he always lives to make intercession for them" (Heb. 7:25). These words I would commend and leave with poor believers that they might have remedy for their comfort as a sufficient consolation for their souls.

A Definition of Faith
To provide a definition for faith, it is a coming to God, by Christ, for salvation. It is coming to be saved. Do not let the desire for assurance that God will save you, or that Christ

is yours, discourage you. It is simply a heart that comes to God, by Christ, to be saved. Remember that the believers in the New Testament are described as those who come to God through Christ. They stop trusting in themselves and rest in nothing within themselves, but rather, they come to God through Christ for salvation, with trembling.

It is a coming to God. He is the ultimate object of our faith and the person with whom we are to believe and from whom we are to receive salvation, if we are to obtain it.

It is a coming to God, by Christ. This phrase is used in Hebrews, as an allusion to the worshipers of the Old Testament, who were directed to go to God by a priest, when they had sinned, who with a sacrifice made an atonement for them. Now, Christ is the great and true high priest by whom we "have access in one Spirit to the Father" (Eph. 2:18). Do you know how to appear before God, or to come to him? Come first to Christ, and he will take you by the hand, go along with you, and lead you to his Father.

It is a coming to God, by Christ, for salvation. Many poor souls are prone to think that in coming to God by faith, it must not aim at itself, or its own salvation. But it must, for this is the purpose faith has in coming to God. And, this is subtly couched within these words from Hebrews 7:25, speaking of the very aim of the heart in coming, "he is able to save."

An Encouragement to Faith

Here is the most vital point of focus: Christ is interceding for souls that are to be saved and for us every day. This is especially valuable for those whose faith is weak. For, when such a soul comes and casts itself upon Christ, the thing in Christ that most fits that action is something which Christ has yet to do for that soul. And as for what has already been done in the past, such a believer's faith is often extremely confused how to come to Christ. For example, when such a person is about to come to God, and he hears of the election of some to salvation from all eternity, because this is an act that has already taken place by God in the past, the person believes casting himself upon God for election is pointless. Likewise, when that person looks upon Christ's death, because it happened in the past, he does not know how to express belief, when he wants assurance that Christ died for him. In reality, he should be coming to Christ to be saved because of his death.

But there is this one work that he still needs to accomplish for us, which he is doing on a daily basis, and that is interceding. For, he ever lives to intercede and pray for us in the strength and merit of the sacrifice he offered up for us. Thus, intercession becomes a suitable object for the aim of a faith that is coming to Christ, or is "to be saved." Those acts of God and Christ which took place in the past coincide more naturally with the faith of assurance. Such a faith receives with comfort that Christ has died for me,

ASSURANCE

has risen again, and is now interceding for me, concluding that I will certainly be saved. This, however, is not the case with a weak faith. Therefore, come to Christ to be saved through his death in the past, and by the merit of it, both for the present and for the time to come. Take your cause in hand, and ask Christ to intercede for you. May the intercession of Christ provide the content needed for your faith to cast itself upon Christ.

Now, if such a soul were to ask, "But will Christ, when I come to him for salvation, be willing to work to intercede for me, and take on my life?" I answer it out of those same words from Hebrews: "He always lives to make intercession for them who draw near to God by him." He lives to intentionally accomplish this work. It is the culmination of his redemptive mission. So if Christ should deny any such soul to take its cause in hand, he must then cease to be a priest. He lives to intercede.

If your soul fears the difficulty of its own particular situation, in respect to the greatness of your sins, and the circumstances surrounding them, to the point that you doubt how you could receive salvation, the apostle further adds, "he is able to save to the uttermost." Regardless of your situation, his intercession knows no bounds. That word, "to the uttermost" is a good word and well placed for our comfort. Take it seriously, because it is a reaching word and extends so far that you cannot look beyond it. Let your soul be set upon the highest mountain that any creature has ever sat upon, so that it is exalted to take in and view the most spacious outlook of sin and misery, and challenges with being saved that any poor, humbled soul has ever experienced. Combine this with all the objections and hindrances of your salvation that the heart of man can imagine or invent. Lift up your eyes and look to the uttermost point you can see, and Christ, by his intercession, is able to save you beyond the horizon and furthest compass of your thoughts, even "to the uttermost" and worst case the heart of man can imagine. For, "the gates of hell shall not prevail against it" (Matt. 16:18).

Once again, consider all that Christ has done in his death to save you and what he continues to do in heaven. If you can imagine having all the saints in heaven and on earth joining together to promote your salvation and praying continuously for you to be saved, how would that encourage you? Can I tell you? One word out of Christ's mouth will do more that all in heaven and earth can do. And how can you know whether Christ has begun to intercede for you? In a word, he has put his Spirit into your heart, and set your own heart to the task of making constant intercessions for yourself (Rom. 8:26). This is the echo of Christ's intercession for you in heaven,

Finally, if such a soul will continue to object, saying "But will he not ever give up on me? Can I not be cast out of his prayers through my unbelief?" Let it be considered here that he lives "ever" to intercede. He intercedes

ASSURANCE

forever, until he has accomplished and finished your salvation. You see, you have the whole life of Christ, first and last, both here and in heaven, laid out for you. He makes your salvation his constant calling. Oh, therefore, let us live completely to him. I conclude with the words of the apostle Paul, "For the love of Christ controls us…that those who live might no longer live for themselves but for him who for their sake died and was raised." (1 Cor. 5:14–15). And there, "he always lives to make intercession for us" (Heb. 7:25).

www.ingramcontent.com/pod-product-compliance
Lightning Source LLC
Chambersburg PA
CBHW072102110526
44590CB00018B/3280